Glaciers

by Mari Schuh

Consulting Editor: Gail Saunders-Smith, PhD

Consultant: Nikki Strong, PhD
St. Anthony Falls Laboratory
University of Minnesota

CAPSTONE PRESS
a capstone imprint

Pebble Plus is published by Capstone Press,
151 Good Counsel Drive, P.O. Box 669, Mankato, Minnesota 56002.
www.capstonepub.com

032010
005740CGF10

Books published by Capstone Press are manufactured with paper containing at least 10 percent post-consumer waste.

Library of Congress Cataloging-in-Publication Data
Schuh, Mari C., 1975–
    Glaciers / by Mari Schuh.
        p. cm.—(Pebble plus. Natural wonders)
    Includes bibliographical references and index.
    Summary: "Simple text and full-color photos explain how glaciers form and why they are an important landform"—
Provided by publisher.
    ISBN 978-1-4296-5006-9 (library binding)
    ISBN 978-1-4296-5594-1 (paperback)
    1. Glaciers—Juvenile literature. I. Title. II. Series.
GB2403.8.S38 2011
551.31'2—dc22   2010002791

Editorial Credits
Katy Kudela, editor; Heidi Thompson, designer; Kelly Garvin, media researcher; Eric Manske, production specialist

Photo Credits
Dreamstime/Jason Cheever, 15; Marcviln, cover; Ndiebold, 21; Nivers, 5; Peter Wollinga, 11; Richard Lindie, 13
Mary Evans Picture Library, 19
Shutterstock/Antoine Beyeler, 7; Dan Breckwoldt, 9; Ramunas Bruzas, 1
Visuals Unlimited/Science VU, 17

Note to Parents and Teachers

The Natural Wonders series supports national geography standards related to the physical and human characteristics of places. This book describes and illustrates glaciers. The images support early readers in understanding the text. The repetition of words and phrases helps early readers learn new words. This book also introduces early readers to subject-specific vocabulary words, which are defined in the Glossary section. Early readers may need assistance to read some words and to use the Table of Contents, Glossary, Read More, Internet Sites, and Index sections of the book.

Table of Contents

How a Glacier Forms 4

On the Move. 10

Famous Glaciers 14

People and Glaciers. 18

Glossary 22

Read More 23

Internet Sites. 23

Index 24

How a Glacier Forms

Snowflakes fall to the ground.

Millions of them pile up

and slowly turn into ice.

The ice grows into a

huge mass called a glacier.

Huge glaciers form near
the North and South Poles.
These wide, thick sheets of ice
spread across the land.
They are continental glaciers.

Valley glaciers are
long rivers of ice.
These smaller glaciers
form in tall mountain areas
around the world.

On the Move

As glaciers grow heavy,

they begin to slowly move.

Glaciers drag rocks and soil.

Over time, the moving ice

carves valleys and canyons.

Some glaciers reach
all the way to the ocean.
Pieces of glacier break off.
The floating ice chunks
become icebergs.

Famous Glaciers

Long ago, glaciers

shaped much of Canada's

Banff National Park.

Today, people visit this park

to see glaciers up close.

15

Alaska has many glaciers.

The state's largest glacier

is the Malaspina Glacier.

It is almost 50 miles

(80 kilometers) wide.

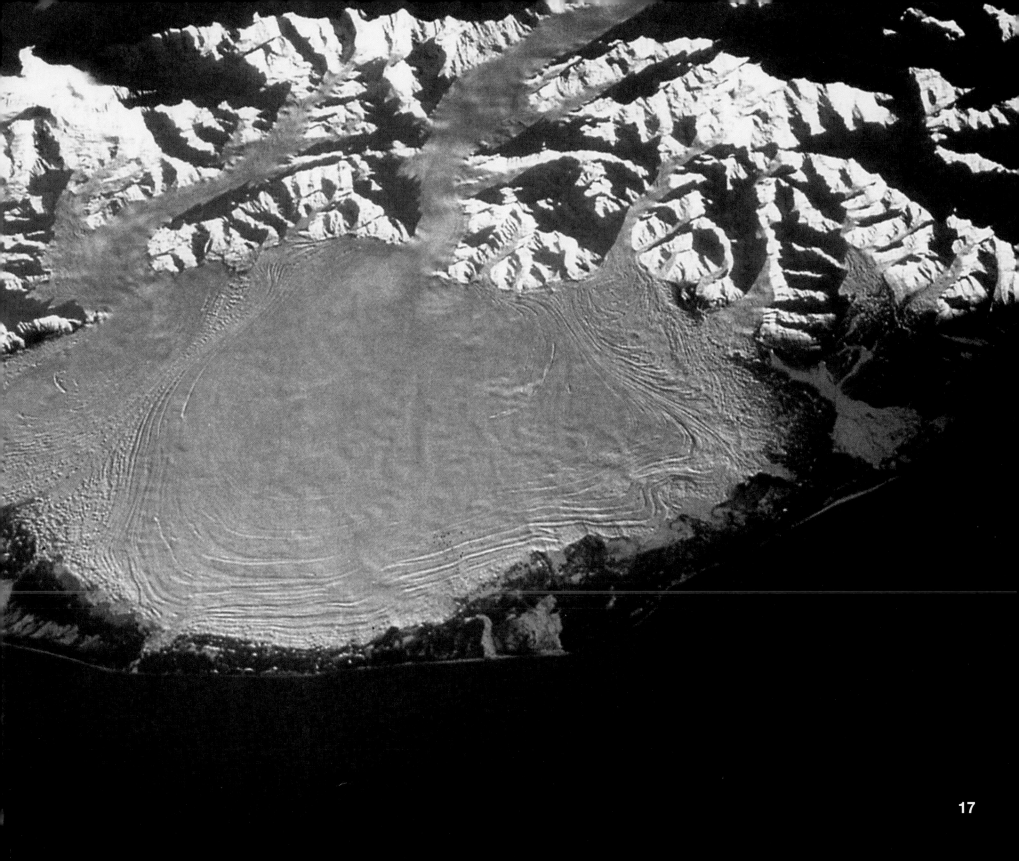

People and Glaciers

During the last ice age,

glaciers covered about

30 percent of Earth's land.

These glaciers left behind

good soil for farming.

Today, melting glaciers give
farmers water for their crops.
People use water from
melting glaciers for
drinking water too.

Glossary

canyon—a deep, narrow river valley with steep sides

continental—part of a continent

ice age—a period of time in history when glaciers covered a large part of Earth

iceberg—a huge mass of ice floating in the sea

mass—a lump or pile of matter that has no particular shape

North Pole—the most northern point on Earth; the North Pole is in the Arctic

South Pole—the most southern point on Earth; the South Pole is at Antarctica

valley—an area of low ground between two hills or mountains; rivers and lakes often form in valleys

Read More

Mis, Melody S. *Exploring Glaciers*. Landforms. New York: PowerKids Press, 2009.

Sepehri, Sandy. *Glaciers*. Landforms. Vero Beach, Fla.: Rourke Pub., 2008.

Internet Sites

FactHound offers a safe, fun way to find Internet sites related to this book. All of the sites on FactHound have been researched by our staff.

Here's all you do:

Visit www.facthound.com

FactHound will fetch the best sites for you!

Index

Banff National Park, 14

canyons, 10

continental glaciers, 6

farming, 18, 20

ice age, 18

icebergs, 12

Malaspina Glacier, 16

melting, 20

mountains, 8

moving, 10

North Pole, 6

rocks, 10

snow, 4

soil, 10, 18

South Pole, 6

valley glaciers, 8

valleys, 10

water, 20

Word Count: 189
Grade: 1
Early-Intervention Level: 24